MAKE YOUR OWN ADVENTURE

LOST IN SLUMBERLAND

Illustrations by Colin Petty
Written by Stewart Cowley

HAMLYN

Published 1985 by
Hamlyn Publishing,
A division of
The Hamlyn Publishing Group Ltd.,
Bridge House, London Road,
Twickenham, Middlesex, England.

Produced for Hamlyn Publishing by
Victoria House Publishing Ltd.,
4/5 Lower Borough Walls,
Bath BA1 1QR, England.

Printed in Belgium.

ISBN 0 600 31054 X

THE ADVENTURE

Wonderful adventures await Bluehat in the strange, magical city of Slumberland – but only you can help him find his way home. He is not sure of the way, and you must make up his mind for him.

As you read the story, you will discover that there are decisions to be made – look for the signposts on the pages. Often there will be two choices, and a different page number beside each one. When you have decided what Bluehat should do, turn to the page number shown, and discover where you have led him!

Have a good adventure, and remember, the choice is yours!

It was a hot summer's day and Bluehat felt very lazy. He sat on a grassy mound in a clearing, watching the sunbeams dancing among the leaves of the forest trees. The soft buzzing of bees among the summer flowers made him feel sleepy. Slowly his eyes closed.

Then he heard the sound of singing and laughter. He opened his eyes with a start, and saw a creaky old waggon rumbling along the track that led through the glade.

Its passengers waved happily to Bluehat as they passed by, but as they disappeared into the trees he saw a small bundle fall off the back and roll into the grass. Bluehat picked it up and called out, but they couldn't hear because he was so far away. He started to run after them.

Bluehat jumped aboard, but everyone was too busy singing to listen to him. He joined in and soon forgot all about the bundle. After a while he saw a beautiful city in the distance, its spires and turrets shining in the sunlight. "I don't remember seeing that place before," he thought as they made their way towards it.

It must have been further away than it looked, for Bluehat eventually fell fast asleep.

When he woke the waggon had reached the city, and had stopped beside a lovely park. But everyone had gone! The bundle he had meant to return was still on the waggon. He didn't know what to do!

Should he wait for his new friends to return, or should he try to look for them?

Bluehat walked away from the park and found himself in a maze of winding, twisting streets. Before long he was completely lost. He was beginning to feel a little frightened when he came to a stout wooden door set into a wall. All sorts of strange banging and clattering noises came from behind it. He was about to open it when he heard a sound above him. He looked up. A large, fluffy cat was sitting on a

ledge just above the doorway, peering at him.

"Welcome to Slumberland," it said. "You look lost. Come up here. Wherever you want to go, I can show you the way."

"I don't know," thought Bluehat. "Cats that talk! What shall I do now?"

Just then an old man covered in clocks and watches stepped up beside him.

"I'm the Clockman. What time is it?" he said, pointing to Bluehat's bundle. Bluehat undid the cloth and found a small red clock inside.

"It just says Time to Sleep," he replied.

"Oh dear, I'm late," said the Clockman. "Quick, follow me." Bluehat hurried along behind until they came to a tall tower with

steps winding up the outside. As they climbed, Bluehat saw rooftops all around. On one of them sat a large, fluffy cat. To his astonishment it spoke.

"Welcome to Slumberland," it whispered. "I'll take you anywhere you want to go."

"Hurry up!" called the Clockman.

Bluehat stepped into a large, steamy kitchen full of bubbling pots and pans. A fat, red-faced cook was rushing about muttering and knocking things over. She stopped when she saw Bluehat.

"Oh good, you're just in time to help me. There is so much to do

for the King's Never-Ending Birthday Party and I'm getting into such a muddle."

"But I'm no good at cooking!" cried Bluehat, backing away hastily towards a door in the corner.

"It doesn't matter," said the cook cheerfully. "They'll be having such a lovely time they'll never know the difference."

At the top of the stairs they stepped into a large, round room filled with the machinery of a giant clock.

"I need help to wind it up," said the Clockman. "You must sit on this weight until it reaches the bottom of that shaft. Then I'll wind you up again." Bluehat climbed nervously onto the weight.

"If I help, will you tell me the way home?" he asked.

"If there's time!" said the Clockman as he pulled a lever. With a

loud clattering, Bluehat sank through the floor and down the shaft. At the bottom he saw a gate leading into a crowded street.

"Come and join us," sang the people in the street happily.

"Up you come!" shouted the Clockman. The chain began to pull Bluehat up again.

"I'm the Cat That Climbs, you know," said the cat. "You'll be safe with me." And with that it set off across the rooftops, stopping every now and then to make sure Bluehat was all right.

Far below, a colourful procession was winding noisily through the streets. The sound of cheerful singing filled the air.

"They're on their way to the Never-Ending Birthday Party," said the cat. "I expect your friends are there. Do you want to join them?"

They were standing by a partly-open window. Bluehat could smell delicious cooking smells coming from inside. The cat began to make its way down to the street.

"Perhaps I should join my friends again," thought Bluehat. "But I do feel hungry and there's something good cooking in there . . ."

"You can make the Surprise Pudding," chuckled the jolly cook. She led Bluehat to a large machine in the corner and left him.

Bluehat didn't know what to do! He poured dozens of eggs, gallons of milk, sugar, nuts and lots of ice-cream into the machine. Then he wiped his hands and pulled the big lever on the side.

"I hope this is right," he muttered to himself.

The machine rumbled and churned, shuddered and burbled,

until huge billows of bubbly pudding began to bulge from every opening. Bluehat tried to hold down the lid, but the Pudding Machine was out of control. The cook had fallen asleep in front of the kitchen fire!

Should he call for help? Or should he creep out of the door?

Bluehat shut the door behind him. "Phew!" he gasped. When he looked around him he found he was in a stable.

"Hello," said a voice that made Bluehat jump.

"Don't be afraid," said another voice. Out of the gloom stepped the strangest creature Bluehat had ever seen. It was a horse with a head at each end!

"Who are you?" asked Bluehat.

"I'm This Way," said one head.

"I'm That Way," said the other. "Can we help you?"

"I'm lost," said Bluehat, and he told This Way That Way his story.

"Well," said That Way, "sit on my back, facing that way, and I'll show you the way into the Never-Ending Birthday Party. Your friends will be there—they will help you."

"Sit on my back, facing this way," said the other head. "I'll take you to the highest hill in the city. You might be able to see your home from there."

"Which way should I go?" laughed Bluehat.

Bluehat was swept up in the throng of happy marchers as they danced and sang through the narrow streets. As he was jostled from group to group, he suddenly found himself among familiar faces. They were some of his friends from the waggon.

"You're just in time to come to the King's Never-Ending Birthday Party," they cried. "Look, we've arrived at the gatehouse!"

A ticket collector stood there scowling.
"But I haven't got a ticket," said Bluehat.
"Slip through the window into the King's gatehouse," whispered one of his friends. "You can find your way from there."
"Or hide under my cloak," said another.

"I think I'll go to the top of the hill," said Bluehat, climbing onto This Way That Way's back. The strange horse trotted to the stable door, pushed it open, and galloped out into the streets of the city. Twisting and turning through a maze of narrow streets, climbing ever higher, the houses they passed became fewer and fewer. At last they came to a grassy hilltop high above the town. There stood a tall tower.

"Well," said This Way. "Can you see your home?" Bluehat searched the horizon, but nothing looked familiar.

"No," he said sadly.

"Told you so," said That Way. "You should go to the party to find your friends. I'll take you there."

"You're just not high enough yet," said This Way. "Climb to the top of the King's Tower. You're sure to see your way home from there." Bluehat was beginning to wonder if he would ever see his home again!

"If you would be so kind," Bluehat said to That Way, "I'd like to try to find my friends at the party."

Bluehat clung tightly to the reins, as That Way galloped up to a tall, green hedge, beyond which lay the King's garden.

"How are we going to get in?" asked Bluehat anxiously.

"Well, this is the quickest way," said That Way, and the little horse leapt lightly over the hedge.

"Hello!" called a voice from the crowd. It was the King's jester,

with bells on his hat and bells on his shoes. He was one of Bluehat's friends from the waggon! Bluehat thanked This Way That Way and followed the jester through the crowd to a gaily decorated stage. As they climbed up, the jester sang . . .

If you help me with the show
Maybe homewards you will go!

Bluehat clung to the chain as it began to lift him up again, but after a while it began to slow and soon stopped altogether. The sound of snoring echoed down the shaft from the room above. Bluehat shouted and whistled but the Clockman was fast asleep. In despair he looked round the solid walls of the shaft and saw a gap in the stone.

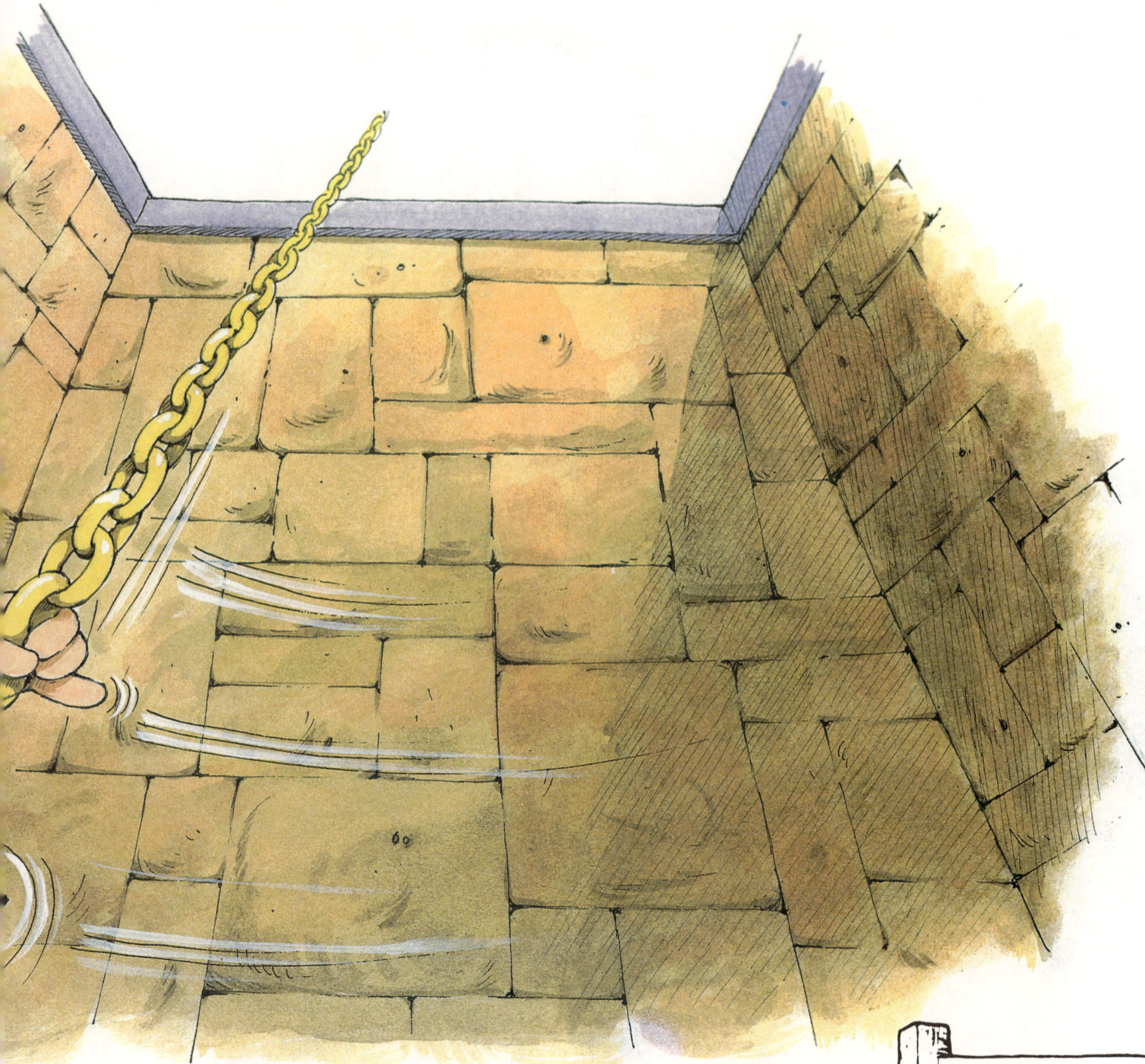

Looking at him through the hole was the Cat That Climbs.

"The Clockman is asleep," cried Bluehat. "What shall I do?"

"What do you expect," yawned the cat. "This is Slumberland! Squeeze through here and come with me."

Taking a deep breath, Bluehat heaved himself through the narrow space and found himself high up on a rooftop beside the cat.

The cook woke up with a start and rushed over to help Bluehat hold the lid down. But it was too late. There was a muffled thump and they were both hurled across the kitchen on a wave of frothing pudding. It carried them right out the door and onto the King's table.

"What a surprising Surprise Pudding," he cried gleefully. "It's the best I've ever had!" He grabbed a huge spoon and waved it at

Bluehat. "Eat as much as you like, little fellow." Then he laughed and said, "But perhaps you've had enough of it and would prefer to play in the Royal Garden."

Bluehat looked out of the window into a huge garden crowded with people.

Bluehat climbed off the table and sat next to the King. The pudding was delicious, but there was so much of it that Bluehat thought he would never stop eating! Suddenly, someone threw a big blob of pudding at Bluehat, but he ducked and it hit the King right on his nose.

"Ho, ho, this means war!" chuckled the King, picking up a custard pie. In an instant, the air was filled with flying food as the biggest

pudding fight in history began.

Bluehat slipped quietly under the table. He was beginning to feel quite tired and sleepy. A little way away he could see a trapdoor set into the floor. He crept towards it, pulled it open and dropped through – just as another custard pie whizzed by.

There was so much going on in the King's garden that Bluehat almost forgot to feel homesick. There were jugglers and acrobats and a fairground where all the rides were free. He was waiting to go on the rollercoaster when a stern-looking guard appeared and placed his hand firmly on Bluehat's shoulder.

"Where is your invitation?" boomed the guard and, taking Bluehat's arm, led him towards the exit.

"Not so fast, Mr. Guard," said a voice from the crowd, and out jumped a familiar figure in the costume of a Jester. "I am the King's Jester, and this young man is my assistant. Come with me, Bluehat."

Bluehat followed the Jester up some steps to a gaily coloured stage. "You can help me do my magic show," he told Bluehat.

The Jester winked at Bluehat, turned to the crowd and bowed. They clapped and cheered at each amazing trick while Bluehat rushed about at the Jester's bidding.

At last the Jester paused and cried, "And now for the finale. I shall make my assistant vanish before your very eyes." He led Bluehat into a large cabinet and drew the curtain.

"Now listen," he said to Bluehat. "When I tap the magic box with

my wand, say these words . . ." And he whispered in Bluehat's ear. Soon, Bluehat heard tap, tap, tap, on the side of the cabinet.

"Oh dear," he thought. "I can't remember the magic words. Did he say Blowy joey crumble and crunch, or Dozey joey crumble and crunch? Which shall I say?"

Bluehat was very tired by the time he had climbed the steps to the top of the tower. There was just one wall, which had a little door in it. The wind howled through. Bluehat could hardly stop himself from being blown away! He crawled towards one of the pillars to look out across the land. A wide ledge ran all around the tower. And there, sitting on the very edge, was the Cat That Climbs.

"You'll see better from here," it called.
"But the wind is so strong," shouted Bluehat. "I might be blown off the edge." He felt so tired, and so cold, all he wanted to do was go to sleep somewhere warm. Perhaps there was shelter behind the little door.

Before he knew what was happening, Bluehat found himself tumbled into a large round room with a large round bed covered in soft, cool, silk pillows.

"Well, I don't seem to be getting any nearer home," sighed Bluehat. And with a great yawn he lay down on the bed. "Perhaps I'll

think of something after a little sleep."

Beside the bed stood a cage in which sang a beautiful golden bird. Bluehat lay on the bed listening to the lovely lullaby – and was fast asleep in no time at all.

A great gust of wind grabbed hold of Bluehat, and before he knew what was happening the wind carried him high into the air. The rooftops of the city soon lay far below. Bluehat shut his eyes until he landed with a thump – and found himself rolling down a familiar grassy mound in his own familiar woods.

"It must all have been a dream," he thought as he rubbed his eyes. "But it seemed so real!" Suddenly a waggon rumbled into the glade

and a small bundle rolled off the back.

"Hey, you've dropped something," he cried as he picked it up and ran after the driver. The waggon stopped and the driver, who wore a funny jester's costume, turned and took it with a big wink and a smile before vanishing into the forest gloom.

THE END

Bluehat woke with a jump to find himself tucked up in his own little bed in his own little house.

"Phew, what a dream that was," he thought. "I wonder what the time can be?" He turned to the table beside the bed, and to his astonishment saw a strange clock where his own used to be. It had no numbers and the hands were on Time to Wake. Beside the little clock lay a single, golden feather and the bell from a jester's cap.

THE END